CW00858032

A poetry chapbook dedicated to victims and families of the ever increasing gun violence in our country and the world.

Cover photo taken by Alfred Harrell at a memorial service held on the grounds of Enon Tabernacle Baptist Church for victims of gun violence in Philadelphia, Pa. September 21, 2013.

Charles Andre Johnson
September 20, 1992-January 13, 2011

What was the initial inspiration for this poetry chapbook?

The murder of a cousin that led to his parents forming a foundation in his name, The CHARLES Foundation, Creating Healthy Alternatives Results in Less Emotional Suffering. The foundation story is as follows: The CHARLES Foundation, http://www.thecharlesfoundation.com/, is a non-profit public charity created to help at risk children. The foundation was created in memory of Charles Andre' Johnson born September 20th, 1992. On January 12, 2011 at 10:40 pm in Philadelphia, Pennsylvania two young men walked up to the car that Charles was sitting in waiting for his sister and opened fire. At 12:55am on January 13th, 2011 Charles Andre' Johnson, 18 years old, died of fatal gunshot wounds at Einstein Hospital. The Philadelphia police found that Charles was killed in a case of mistaken identity by two young men 23 and 25 years old with previous criminal arrest records. Prior to his death, Charles worked full time in the family business. He worked every day caring for over 100 chronically mentally ill adults. Charles had also applied to go to school for carpentry. Charles had a son, Khalif twenty-six days after his death.

This foundation was created and implemented by Charles' parents, brother, two sisters and fiancé. It was created to provide advocacy and assist children with skills and self-esteem building and conflict resolution in an attempt to reduce violence and murder in our communities and among the youth. We are working with a variety of grassroots and community organizations to reduce violence. It is our hope and prayer that this foundation will be the basis of recovery and redemption for many so that they do not end up dead or in prison.-The CHARLES Foundation (The aforementioned text is the The CHARLES Foundation 2013 gala brochure)

Thirty percent of the profits generated from paperback copy sales of this chapbook will be split 3 ways with 10% being given to each of the following organizations: Charles Foundation, http://www.thecharlesfoundation.com/, North Carolinians Against Gun Violence, http://www.ncgv.org/ and Parents Against Gun Violence, http://www.parentsagainstgunviolence.com/, to support their ongoing efforts to bring awareness to the rising tide of gun violence and their efforts in working for reasonable not necessarily anti-second amendment legislation to reduce gun violence in our nation.

The decision to donate part of the profits of this book is a personal one because I believe change comes through community efforts not the efforts of one individual or organization.

Alfred Harrell-Inspirational Speaker, Poet, Activist

Table of Contents

Night Angels

Under the darkness of night angels born of men rise and fall like shooting stars traveling the open range of the heavens with their tails of fiery light turning dark to dawn as they reach for the fingertips of God

Defiant Voices

Armed to the hip our country is
Parents bear the broken bleeding bodies of the children in their arms
Our politicians pass blame like they pass useless laws
Filled with loop holes while bullets leap through the air
Leaving holes in the innocent
Religious leaders preach funerals filled with empty ideologies
Such as God needed another angel
Such as it was Gods will
Willfully they miss apply the words of wise King Solomon
As too times and seasons for everything under the sun
Something has to be done since Lady Justice only cries
Wields her sword and balances her scales
When children who look like her dies
Her blindfold barely rises to Black on Black crime
Her swords swings swiftly when it is her kind
Her scales are balanced when children who look like her bleed
Armed to the hip our country is
Parents bear the broken bleeding bodies of the children in their arms
Our politicians pass blame like they pass useless laws
Filled with loop holes while bullets leap through the air
Leaving holes in the innocent
Defiant voices must rise
Defiant voices must rise
Defiant voices must rise
Resurrect hope
Bury hopelessness
Hold candlelight vigils
Lead a social revolution
Revolving around winds of lasting change
Unlock the mental locks of our nation
Our nation that spends more on war than education
Educating the masses that it is more than Black on Black crime

It is about the blood of Columbine
It is about the blood of Trayvon Martin
It is about the blood covered movie goers in Colorado
Defiant voices must rise
Until Lady Justice's blindfold is sandblasted
Until her eyes weep an ocean of tears
Until her sword brings justice like a vigilante blade
Until her scales are finally balanced
By the raining teardrops of all loving fathers and mothers

Parental Cries

Dark nights rise over human skies
Desperate sacrificial offerings are laid at Lady Justice feet
Demanding reasonable solutions
Before the pale rider of the Apocalypse
Touches another college campus
Virginia Tech
Touches another school
Lines at another Columbine and Newtown Elementary
Touches another movie night
Colorado...Dark Knight Rises
Touches another hooded teens life
When a Paul Blart mall cop wannabe
Brings a gun to a rock fight
When will enough be...enough
When will we realize all of us...bleed
When bullets dance through the air leaving holes in the innocent
Our preachers
Our psychologists
Our politicians
Offer us sugar filled placebos
Sweets craftily designed to drive us into diabetic comas
So that we will momentarily lose our collective consciousness
Dip into dreams served up by the Sandman
Dreams nightmares delivered to us by the Boogieman
Dark nights continue rising over human skies
Distraught parents cry
Drop their tears upon the altars of unfulfilled dreams
Parental cries fall like rain from human skies
Parental cries scream for a new social revolution
Parental cries respect the right to bear arms

Problem is

Preachers and politicians promote fear

Problem is

People don't rise from the dead like in video game

Truth is

When victim and villain dies

Another

Parent cries

Vanishing

As this poem is being read bullets needlessly rocket out of a guns barrel
As this poem is being read a child is being buried in our Earth's soil
As this poem is being read a parent tears fall like a rapidly flowing river
As this poem is being read a final kiss good-bye floats heavenward
As this poem is being another Black child vanished like smoke in the wind
Our days are like Frederick Douglas days
Wounds of racism permeate America's soul
Our days are like Martin's, Medgar's and Malcolm's day
Injustice flows through America's consciousness
Our are days are like the days of the Civil Rights Movement
Militarized police still pounce upon peaceful protesters
Our days are Ferguson, Missouri
Our days are the streets of New York City
Our days are a playground in Cleveland, Ohio
Our days are a 9 year old playing outside in Chicago, Illinois
Our days are Baltimore, Maryland burning for justice
Injustice screams loudly like cracks of thunder before a summer rain storm
Lady Justice plugs up her ears
Words of media paid hate-mongers fuel fabricated fears
Force intolerance into an unmarked grave
Our children are dying upon playgrounds turned into battlefields
Their blood trickling through cracks of asphalt
While words of hope drown in a cesspool of failed government policies
Our Black children are dying vanishing like raindrops bouncing upon hot pavement
Our Black children are dying at the hands of police officers trained in the art of war
Our Black children are being laid to rest forever by the god named: stand your ground
Our Black children are dying from Black on Black crime
Our children lives are vanishing like smoke in the wind
Our children are dying
Vanishing like raindrops touching hot asphalt

The Blindfold Falls

Lady Liberty holds Lady Justice in a chokehold
She speaks gasping for air, "I can't breathe"
Breathless she lays limp on concrete slab, sidewalk
Death of the Apocalypse claims her soul
America cries
Black America cries
Mexican America cries
White America cries
Hispanic America cries
Jewish America cries
Arab America cries
A nations of immigrants cries for justice
And another Grand Jury fails to indict
Another it's justified killing it determines
And the blindfold never falls from the eyes of Lady Justice

Together We Heal

An inspirational speech By Alfred Harrell Copyright 2015

The 2015 theme of Triad Poetry Meetup 100 Thousand Poets for Change Event September 26, 2015

Perhaps if I was blind I would see no evil in my world, if I was deaf perhaps I would hear no hurtful sounds, if I was mute perhaps I would speak no harmful words, if my mind was blind perhaps I would not have judgmental thoughts of others however since I'm not physically or mentally challenged in any of those ways the best can I can do is utilize my vision to find ways to heal the issues facing my family, community and world at large. Perhaps, just perhaps after you leave here today… you will leave here with a clearer vision as to how you can become a greater catalyst for healing within your family and community.

We could spend hours discussing some of the hotly debated and protested issues facing us all: issues such as racism, equal educational opportunities, police brutality and the rising tide of gun violence which knows no cultural, ethnic, political or religious boundaries. These issues as well as others impact each one of us either directly or indirectly however time will not permit us to address them in detail and since it does not we will focus upon possible ways we can work together for healing within our families and community.

Guitarist Jerry Cantrell once said, **"Part of the healing process is sharing with other people who care."** When we share our opinions about things that bother us to the very core of our souls with others in a non-confrontational setting we may discover a higher level of humanity in own self and in the person or persons with whom we are engaging in a conversation.

    One of the first steps to healing together is open non-judgmental conversation; pro-actively listening to learn a different viewpoint

    Another step is sharing points of view about the issue at hand in a non-condescending way

    A third way is being willing to accept the common ground on the issue under discussion if there is one or simply agree to disagree. You and I, we have to challenge ourselves not to hold on to a preconceived or presently held devise harmful viewpoint: George Bernard Shaw said **"Progress is impossible without change, and those who cannot change their minds cannot change anything."**

None of us can truly walk in another person's shoes or feel another person's pain however what we can do is make a conscious daily effort to work for healing on a personal level with regards to issues in own intimate circle or our community.

What we can do is choose not to be part of the devise hate-baiting elements of our society whether they be the media, politics or religion.

What we can choose to be...we must choose to be are forces for healing within our community by making sure our vision is one of healing together with others.

In conclusion Leroy Hood once said, **"Don't underestimate the power of your vision to change the world. Whether that world is your office, your community, an industry or a global movement, you need to have a core belief that what you contribute can fundamentally change the paradigm or way of thinking about problems."**

Quotes from the website: http://www.brainyquote.com

Discussion questions for families, community action groups and religious groups concerned about rising gun violence in our nation.

Have you or anyone you know been a victim of gun violence because of the easy access to firearm?

What do you think if anything could have prevented that access?

Do we as a nation need stricter laws governing access to firearms? Would stricter laws be an infringement upon our second amendment rights? Why are gun locks good safety devices when there are children residing with gun owners?

What might stem the rising tide of gun violence from those with mental health issues and persons identified to be living in domestic violence prone situations by public authorities?

What might be done to limit access to firearms by the criminal elements in our communities?

Are body cameras good deterrents to the usage of lethal force by means of a firearm for members of law enforcement as they carry out their sworn duty to protect and serve all members of our society?

As a non-firearm owner or as a firearm owner what good or bad is accomplished through one on one or group discussions about the impact of gun violence upon our community and nation?

Would better educational programs along with national background ground checks when it omes all gun shows and local or private gun sellers reduce to number of firearm related deaths in your opinion?

Personal Notes

Personal Notes

Personal Notes

North Carolinians Against Gun Violence Reference Materials

http://www.ncgv.org/

Gun locks are one of the best tools to prevent youth firearm suicide. This video demonstrates how to use a standard cable lock.
Gun locks are available for free at many local Sheriff and Health Departments. If you need help finding a gun lock contact us at 919.403.7665 or NCGV@NCGV.org
If you, or someone you know, is in suicidal crisis or emotional distress please call 1-800-273-TALK (8255)
If you are a veteran in distress, please call the national veterans suicide crisis line 1-800-273-8255) you will be connected to a VA specific line so you will speak to someone who understands.

Other Resources

American Foundation for Suicide Prevention- general information about suicide

Triangle Consortium for Suicide Prevention-Triangle resource for getting active in suicide prevention and Triangle support groups

National Mental Health Association- Information and help

ReachOut - A place for teens to talk with other teens

National Institute of Mental Health- Statistics and Prevention

SPRC- North Carolina State Suicide Prevention Information

It Get's Better Project - Provides support to LGBT youth and youth being bullied
To find out more about the difference you can make in a friend or loved one's life, visit http://www.whatadifference.org/

Healthy Mind and Body, A Resource Guide to Suicide Prevention - Thanks to the Girl Scout Troop from Seattle who thought this would be a helpful resource!

It's ok 2 Ask about youth suicide prevention
Save a Life A teen suicide awareness program

14

Know the Facts About Suicide and Guns

In North Carolina teens often make the impulsive decision to end their lives. When provided easy access to a firearm it is almost always a permanent and deadly decision. In North Carolina more than 50% of all firearm deaths are suicides (2007 Data WISQARS**

In North Carolina suicide is the 2nd leading cause of violent death for adolescents (2007 Data WISQARS)

49 % of youth suicides in North Carolina involve a firearm—the largest chosen method (2007 Data WISQARS)

Many youth suicides are impulsive. A study of youth under 18 who attempted suicide found one-third who attempted suicide made the decision on the same day and in many cases the same hour (Harvard School of Public Health)

In a study of firearm suicide survivors, the majority stated 'availability' as the reason they chose a gun (Harvard School of Public Health)

A National Violent Injury Statistics System(NVISS) Study of firearm suicides among youth under 18 found that 82% used a firearm belonging to a family member, usually a parent. When storage status was noted, about two-thirds of the firearms had been stored unlocked (Harvard School of Public Health)

In the above study, among the remaining cases, in which the firearms had been locked, the youth either knew the combination or where the key was kept, or broke into the cabinet where one or more firearms were stored. (Harvard School of Public Health)
Firearm suicide is significantly more fatal than other means. More than 90 percent of suicide attempts with a gun are fatal. In comparison, only 3 percent of attempts with drugs or cutting are fatal (Harvard School of Public Health)

Suicide death isn't inevitable. A study of individuals who attempted suicide and survived found that nine out of ten did not die by suicide at a later date. (Owens 2002)
<u>Reducing at-risk youth's access to firearms has been proven to reduce their risk of suicide death and yet. . .</u>

In a recent study 45% of North Carolina gun owners with children in the home report leaving their weapons unlocked and 36% report leaving the weapon loaded
More than 168,000 children and teens in North Carolina live in homes with loaded guns
More than 82,000 live in homes with guns that are loaded*and* unlocked

In a study among gun-owning parents who reported that their children had never handled their firearms at home, 22% of the children, questioned separately, said that they had. (Baxley F, Miller M. 2006)

Lightning Source UK Ltd.
Milton Keynes UK
UKRC012120280519
343495UK00006B/135